# C
# MUSIC

Almost daily, a unique and ancient tradition is performed in Britain's historic cathedrals: the choral service. As the choir lifts its voice in prayer, singing works from the past and the present, the sacred space echoes with the heavenly sound, lifting the heart and freeing the spirit. This heritage of church music, one of Britain's greatest treasures, is now at its most glorious. The cathedrals welcome you to draw near and listen.

*'O sing unto the Lord a new song,
for he hath done marvellous things.'*
PSALM 98, V: 1

# CATHEDRAL MUSIC TODAY

BRITAIN'S CATHEDRALS and college chapels have a unique tradition of choral music that is admired by choirmasters across the globe. Daily, music is performed to an exquisitely high standard in religious establishments throughout the country, and what is extraordinary is that this has been happening for many hundreds of years, with a brief pause of 15 years prior to the Restoration of the Monarchy in 1660.

Christian worship has always made great use of music to enhance and enrich its power, though this has not always been met with approval. St Augustine (354–430) confessed: 'Whenever it happens that I am more moved by the singing than by the thing that is sung, I admit that I have grievously sinned', while St John Chrysostom (*c*.347–407) raged: 'Thus does the devil stealthily set fire to the city, [using] degraded music, and songs full of all kinds of wickedness.'

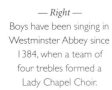

— *Right* —
Boys have been singing in Westminster Abbey since 1384, when a team of four trebles formed a Lady Chapel Choir.

— *Above* —
Full of excitement and raring to go, seven little girls start their probationary year before becoming choristers at Salisbury.

— *Right* —
The choir of Christ Church Cathedral, Oxford. The cathedral's first organist was the composer John Taverner, who was appointed by Cardinal Wolsey in 1526.

Well-performed music engages with the emotions and lifts the words that are being sung to a greater height. It can also help in conveying the meaning of a text. However, the music is not only an aid to worship, but also a positive act of worship in itself, performed by the accomplished choir on behalf of the congregation.

## THE MUSIC STAFF

The Precentor has overall responsibility for the cathedral's music. He produces an outline for each service but relies on the organists to add appropriate choral pieces. It is usually the Precentor who sings the first line of each of the responses during a service. The Organist and Director of Music oversees the preparation and execution of the music, and during services will either conduct the choir or play the organ. He is helped by an Assistant Organist. The organists spend many hours practising the organ, preparing scores, and managing and developing the repertoire.

*— Left —*
The organist
Andrew Lumsden
playing the organ
at Winchester.

Choral services are sung following the ancient choral rules of the Church of England, which were founded on the Latin services used in this country before the Reformation. Visitors today can attend a service of choral Evensong on most weekdays. Sunday's services of choral Mattins, Eucharist and Evensong will include congregational hymns and a sermon. Those unable to attend in person can tune in to BBC Radio 3 on Wednesdays at 4 p.m. for the weekly Choral Evensong, which has been broadcast live since 1926.

*— Above —*
This green man, carved in the
congregational stalls of Winchester
Cathedral's quire, brings a smile to
the face of many a visitor.

# THE CHORAL TRADITION

BRITAIN'S CHORAL TRADITION is rooted in the cathedrals' monastic foundations. Monks would chant the choral offices eight times a day, and boys who resided in the monasteries – novices, relatives and servants – would sometimes join them. During the 12th century many Lady Chapels were built, and it was considered fitting to employ boy singers for their gentle, more feminine sound. Gradually, over the next three centuries as polyphony (music with different parts sung simultaneously) developed, the boys began to sing with the men.

By the beginning of the 16th century, at least 50 English monasteries and abbeys maintained choirs, but these were swept away when the monasteries were dissolved in 1536–40. A few musicians found work in Henry VIII's 'cathedrals of the new foundation'.

4

— *Below* —
St David's Cathedral, like many others, has misericords in the quire. These little ledge seats, made for monks to lean on during long services, are carved with grotesque and humorous motifs.

The first Prayer Book, introduced in 1549, specified that worship, previously elaborate and in Latin, should now be simple, straightforward and 'understanded of the people'. This meant that all the Latin settings had to be changed to English – except in college chapels, where Latin, the language of scholars, could be understood. The eight ancient 'Hours of Prayer' were replaced by the two offices of Morning and Evening Prayer, and while the Psalter (the Book of Psalms) had previously been recited through once a week, it was now to be spread over a month – a practice that continues in cathedrals to this day.

— *Left* —
Monks sang eight choral offices each day: Vigil, Lauds, Prime, Terce, Sext, None, Evensong or Vespers, and Compline.

— *Left* —
Many of Lichfield's vicars choral live in the pretty Vicar's Close that was originally built for them in the 15th century.

The English Civil War (1642–9) spelled disaster for cathedral music. The Puritans, opposed to the beauty and richness of ritual in cathedral worship, pillaged the cathedrals, hacked the organs to pieces, destroyed music books and disbanded the choirs. For 15 years churches knew no music, other than dull, Puritanical psalm singing.

The monarchy was reinstated in 1660, when Charles II was proclaimed king, and initial steps were taken to re-establish the Church of England. A new Prayer Book was published in 1662. Once the cathedrals had addressed the huge problem of rebuilding and retraining their choirs and recovering the choral tradition, cathedral music flourished and grew until about 1700.

But in the 18th century there was a shameful lapse in the spiritual life of the Anglican Church. While senior clergy indulged in the high life, music was given no money and the standards degenerated to a deplorable level. The numbers of choirmen fell, in some provincial cathedrals to only one! The organists themselves were often completely incompetent, and the music was rarely rehearsed. Anthems and services calling for many voices fell into disuse, and the repertoire was reduced to a mere handful of pieces, used in rotation.

Choristers suffered terribly at this time. Many were boarded out with local clergy and other officials, who exploited them in the lowest menial chores. They received very little education, and were poorly fed and clothed. In 1811 Miss Maria Hackett began campaigning for the boys of St Paul's and, having secured better care for them, inspected and monitored conditions at every cathedral in England and Wales.

— *Left* —
An old custom at Salisbury involves every newly admitted boy chorister having his head bumped on a well-worn stone in the Choir Aisle. Today this is anticipated with excitement, but in the past it was something to be dreaded!

— *Above* —
For over 50 years, Maria Hackett visited and revisited the cathedrals to check their provisions for choristers. She hounded them with letters if she had a complaint.

— *Above* —
The choir of Lincoln Cathedral, c.1850, with its organist and master of the choristers, John Young, on the occasion of his retirement. Mr Young held the post for 45 years and significantly improved the quality of the music.

— *Below* —
The choir of King's College, Cambridge, is world-famous, particularly for its broadcast Festival of Nine Lessons and Carols at Christmas.

The 19th-century organist and composer Samuel Sebastian Wesley fought vehemently to save cathedral music, but its eventual recovery was brought about by the Oxford Movement (1833–45). This was an intellectual movement whose emphasis was on ritual and ceremony, and newly ordained curates under its influence, including the ardent Walter Kerr Hamilton, were soon revitalizing the worship in parish churches. In 1841 The Reverend Hamilton became Precentor at Salisbury Cathedral and immediately set about raising the standard of the music, applying fines for non-attendance of choirmen and scheduling regular practices. The results were emphatic and other cathedrals gradually followed suit.

— *Above* —
The head chorister and a probationer from Wells Cathedral's girls choir. In most choirs, a probationer is given a white surplice when he or she becomes a full chorister.

— *Above* —
A young Lincoln chorister takes a rest in the cathedral before a service.

Until recent years this rich choral tradition has remained entirely male, but today more and more cathedrals are introducing girl choristers. As well as giving girls the opportunity to share in the rare privilege of cathedral music, this can relieve the burden of duty on the boys. This remains a controversial issue, and cathedrals are undertaking the change with great care so that the precious tradition of boy choristers is not lost.

— *Below* —
Parents of Guildford choristers, whose school is 5.5km (3½ miles) from the cathedral, have calculated that their combined driving miles in a year would take them the circumference of the globe!

Today, the cathedrals appoint organists and choirmasters of the highest calibre, who, as Wesley put it, are 'men consecrated by their genius, and set apart for duties which only the best talent of the kind can adequately fulfil.' As a result, the musical standards are higher now than ever before.

# THE CHOIRS

ALTHOUGH BRITAIN'S cathedral, chapel and abbey choirs vary in size, most consist of a front row of boy or girl choristers who sing the treble line, and a back row of adult male singers (called lay clerks, lay vicars or vicars choral) who sing the alto, tenor and bass lines. The choir is traditionally divided between two sides, known as Decani: the south side containing the Dean's stall, and Cantoris: the north side containing the Precentor's stall. These sides chant the verses of the psalms antiphonally (alternately) and, when the trebles divide into two parts, Decani takes the higher part and Cantoris the lower. Each choir will have head and deputy head choristers who will wear medals of office, and possibly a number of senior choristers.

*— Below —*
The Winchester choristers walk from their school in the close over to the cathedral for Evensong.

*— Right —*
A Truro chorister puts on his ruff, cassock and white surplice before a service.

## OXFORD AND CAMBRIDGE

The Oxbridge college chapel choirs are made up of male student choral scholars in the back row, and boy choristers or female student choral scholars in the front row. With shorter terms and less pressure than the cathedral choirs, they can achieve very high standards and produce an adventurous repertoire. They are, in effect, the seedbeds of church music, and produce many of our greatest organists and choir directors.

Most cathedrals have an associated choir school close by, dedicated to providing board, care and education for the choristers along with other non-singing pupils, and these often occupy fine historic buildings in the cathedral close. Some choirs have their schools further away, and others draw their choristers from local schools.

— *Above* —
The choir of New College, Oxford, was established in 1379, when William of Wykeham made provision for 16 choristers and a number of clerks to sing daily offices in his fine new chapel.

— *Right* —
Choristers get used to making the most of their free time. Here some boys from Canterbury are seen playing with go-karts outside their boarding house.

— *Left* —
Some Ely choristers pose menacingly with the devil outside Marienkirche in Lübeck, Germany, while on tour with the choir.

# THE CHOIRS

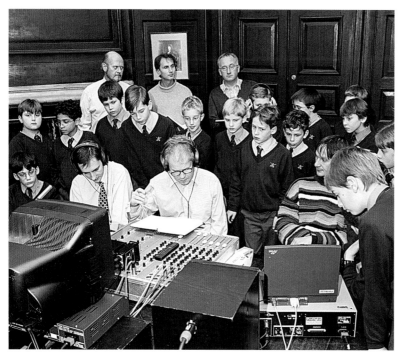

**BEYOND THE CATHEDRAL**
Cathedral choirs like to share what they do with the diocese (the district under the pastoral care of the Bishop) by singing Evensong in the parish churches from time to time, and with the wider world by performing concerts, taking part in broadcasts, recording CDs and going on tour. Some senior choristers are extremely well travelled!

*— Above —*
During a recording session, the choir of St Paul's checks the results in the sound room.

*— Right —*
A Carlisle chorister walks where many a chorister has walked before him – by the Salkeld Screen, erected in 1541.

A cathedral choir is always up against time, and this is reflected in the choristers' daily life. Monday to Saturday, the typical chorister will wake in his school dormitory and rise early for a morning choir practice. After the day's lessons (between which are slotted instrumental tuition and practices) he will process to the cathedral for a practice and Evensong. Tea is followed by prep (homework) and bed. On Sundays he might sing three services, but will have some time to spend with his parents in between. The choristers stay at school for Easter and Christmas.

This highly disciplined life sounds like relentlessly hard work, but most choristers revel in the sheer variety of the demands made upon them. The friendships formed between the boys are deep, as is their sense of purpose and achievement. But it is often not until a chorister has become an adult that he can look back and see the huge benefits of his extraordinary childhood. Having experienced the discipline of singing daily to a meticulously high standard in a self-critical team, he will have gained confidence, application, focus, a fundamental understanding of music, and skills in personal organisation. Above all he will have sung marvellous music in a magnificent building, playing his part in the progress of a unique tradition.

10

Choristers are selected at voice trials. The quality they most need is a 'good ear' – the ability to pick out notes from a chord, sing back melodies and so on – as this will determine how well a child will sing in tune and learn new music. A clear voice will be an advantage, but an enthusiasm for singing is essential. Choral directors also look for a child who can focus on the task in hand, and one with the character to cope with the many demands.

*— Below —*
Members of the Canterbury choir relax during a photo shoot outside their cathedral.

*— Above —*
The adult singers of Christ Church Cathedral, Oxford, are made up of six undergraduates of Christ Church college (academic clerks) and six professional singers (lay clerks).

*'Wherefore with my utmost art*
*I will sing thee.'*
GEORGE HERBERT (1593–1632)

*— Right —*
After a football match, the headmaster of Polwhele House, Truro, ensures that his choristers get back to Evensong with dry feet!

### ETON AND WINCHESTER
Eton College is well known for its fine chapel choir, which has sung since the chapel's completion in 1487. Many of the choir are ex-cathedral choristers, who have won music scholarships to Eton.
The boy trebles of Winchester College's chapel choir are known as Quiristers. They were first brought together in the 1390s, at the foundation of the college, and their early duties included waiting at table. They are now educated at The Pilgrims' School, along with the cathedral choristers.
Some Eton and Winchester College services are open to the public.

# THE ORGANS

THE FIRST ORGAN of which any detailed record exists was erected in Winchester Cathedral in the 10th century. It was a monstrous machine with 400 pipes, which needed two men to play it and 70 men to blow it, and was so loud it could be heard throughout the city. Instead of keys, such organs had cumbersome wooden sliders that the players pushed in and pulled out, one at a time, to admit wind to the pipes.

*— Above —*
The organ has always been associated with Christian worship, and was well established in England by the year 800.

From 1400 organ building became a specialized craft, and great developments were made. But at the Dissolution, many London organs were removed, or silenced and left to decay. Worse was to come during the Civil War, when the Puritans hacked many organs to pieces. It was not that they objected to the organ itself, but just to its use in public worship. In fact, Cromwell had the organ of Magdalen College, Oxford, taken down and rebuilt at his own home at Hampton Court.

*— Above —*
Father Henry Willis (1821–1901) built the organs at many British cathedrals, including Canterbury, Coventry, Exeter, Hereford, Gloucester, St Paul's, Christ Church and Wells.

Few new organs were built in England at this time, and some important builders, including Robert Dallam, Thomas Harris and 'Father' Bernard Smith, took their skills to Europe. When the monarchy was reinstated in 1660 the builders were inundated with work. Renatus Harris (son of Thomas) and Father Smith returned from Europe, bringing new ideas and techniques to English organ building. In 1710 Harris built a four-manual organ at Salisbury, with 46 stops. Pedals, first added to English organs in 1726, only gained acceptance a hundred years later through the work of Father Henry Willis.

*— Below —*
A chorister receives an organ lesson at Gloucester Cathedral. Many of today's choristers are the organists and composers of the future.

*'Loud organs, his glory*
*Forth tell in deep tone,*
*And sweet harp, the story*
*Of what he hath done.'*
SIR HENRY W. BAKER (1821–77)

When the organ became popular for the performance of operatic and orchestral pieces, the 'romantic' organ was developed, with stops imitating orchestral instruments. Although powerful and atmospheric, these were unsuited to the baroque music preferred in the mid 20th century, and in 1954 a Harrison organ was built at London's Royal Festival Hall capable of playing both romantic and baroque works. This set the trend for builders countrywide.

Today there are many fine and historic organs to discover in Britain's cathedrals, each built to suit the acoustic and architecture of its own building. You can hear the organ at most choral services, but also at other times of day when the organist is practising.

# THE MUSIC

WEEKDAY CHORAL EVENSONG will include the proper psalms for the day, a setting of the evening canticles (Magnificat and Nunc Dimittis) and an anthem, as well as readings and prayers. Sunday services – Eucharist (Holy Communion), Mattins and Evensong – are likely to include hymns and a sermon. Eucharist features a setting of the mass and possibly a motet. Mattins is similar to Evensong but the canticles sung are usually the Te Deum and Jubilate (Psalm 100).

*— Above —*
An embroidery at Wells, situated behind the Canon Precentor's stall, depicts King David, the psalmist.

*— Left —*
A window at Chichester illustrates Psalm 150: 'Praise him in the sound of the trumpet; praise him upon the lute and harp.'

## THE PSALMS

The Book of Psalms is divided into 60 sections, one to be recited or sung on the morning and evening of each day of the month. The psalms are sung to Anglican chants: the chant accommodates two verses of the psalm, and the psalm is 'pointed' in such a way that it can be sung in speech-rhythm. Sometimes a Gregorian plainsong chant is used.

With monthly repetition, the singers grow to know and love the psalms like old friends. Particular favourites are the psalms of the reflective 4th evening ('The Lord is my shepherd, therefore can I lack nothing'); the tender and imploring 8th ('Like as the hart desireth the water-brooks, so longeth my soul after thee O God'); and the long and fiery 78th ('He smote their cattle also with hailstones, and their flocks with hot thunderbolts').

*— Right —*
Two young Winchester choristers look through the pointing of the psalm before Evensong.

## THE ANTHEM

The anthem is a uniquely English art form, considered almost obligatory in cathedral services today. It is chosen for its suitability to the church season, and is sung after the collects (prayers), providing a moment for personal reflection.

## THE EVENING CANTICLES

English composers have written settings for the Magnificat and Nunc Dimittis (sometimes known as Services) since the introduction of the first Prayer Book in 1549, and these now form a considerable body of music. The two are always set in the same key, and known by the name of the composer, and either the key (Stanford in C) or the cathedral for which it was written (Howells Gloucester). The Magnificat is the song of praise of the Virgin Mary and the Nunc Dimittis the valedictory song of the old man Simeon.

## THE MASS

Innumerable settings of the mass have been written by composers of all European countries. Usually sung in Latin, the passages set for choirs are: Kyrie, Gloria, Credo, Sanctus, Benedictus and Agnus Dei.

## THE CHURCH CALENDAR

Advent
Christmas Day: 25 December
Epiphany: 6 January
Candlemas: 2 February
Ash Wednesday: February/March
Lent
Mothering Sunday
Passiontide
Maundy Thursday
Good Friday
Easter Day: March/April
Ascension Day: May
Pentecost (Whit Sunday): May/June
Trinity Sunday: June
All Saints' Day: 1 November
All Souls' Day: 2 November

WESTMINSTER ABBEY, St Paul's Cathedral and
St George's Chapel, Windsor, have very special responsi-
bilities in hosting services for all royal and state events.

Westminster Abbey has been the venue for almost
every coronation since 1066, including that of Her
Majesty Queen Elizabeth II on 2 June 1953. The Abbey
was closed for five months prior to the event in order that
preparations could be made. As The Queen and her
procession entered, the choir sang Hubert Parry's anthem,
'I was glad when they said unto me, we will go into the
House of the Lord'. Coronations are held before the high
altar, and performed by the Archbishop of Canterbury.

The magnificent cathedral of St Paul's has hosted many
events of great national importance. Services of thanksgiving and celebration have been held here, such as royal
jubilees and the 100th birthday of Her Majesty Queen
Elizabeth the Queen Mother, and services of great solem-
nity, including the state funerals of Nelson, the Duke of
Wellington and Gladstone.

— *Above* —
The coronation of Queen Victoria, held at
Westminster Abbey in 1837.

— *Below* —
The state funeral of Admiral Lord Nelson was held
at St Paul's Cathedral in 1806. The national hero's
body was delivered to St Paul's by barge.

Situated in the Lower Ward of Windsor
Castle, the historic chapel of St George is
the burial place of ten monarchs. It was
founded in 1475 as the chapel of the Order
of the Garter. The banners of the Knights
of the Garter hang above the magnificent
carved woodwork of the quire, and behind
the stalls can be seen some 670 stall plates
of previous knights, including that of
Sir Winston Churchill.

16

## THE CHAPEL ROYAL

The Chapel Royal is not a place, but a body of clergy and musicians (including the 'Gentlemen' and 'Children' of the choir) whose purpose is to serve the spiritual needs of the sovereign. They are based at the chapel of St James's Palace, London. Many of England's finest composers were employed in the Chapel Royal, records of which go back to 1135. The choir held a very high standard. When the monarchy was reinstated in 1660 there were few experienced trebles available, so the choir-master invoked an ancient press-gang warrant and raided the cathedrals and collegiate choirs of their best boy singers. Services at the royal chapels of Hampton Court and the Tower of London are sung by independent choirs.

*— Left —*
HRH the Duchess of Gloucester, patron of the Friends of St Paul's.

*— Right —*
On Garter Day, each June, HM The Queen and 24 Knights, dressed in robes of the Garter, process from the Upper Ward of Windsor Castle to St George's Chapel for a service of thanksgiving.

# THE COMPOSERS

JOHN TAVERNER was amongst the first composers of music for the Anglican Church. He wrote music for Latin texts in the early 16th century, and is believed to have adapted two of his masses into English, in anticipation of the Reformation.

When the Church was reformed in 1549, Christopher Tye, Thomas Tallis and the other composers of the time were given just five months to produce musical settings for the new English liturgy. Bishop Cranmer prescribed that they should be not 'full of notes, but ... for every sylla-ble a note, so that it may be sung distinctly and devoutly'.

Amongst the late 16th- and early 17th-century composers that followed were Thomas Morley, Thomas Tomkins, Thomas Weelkes, Orlando Gibbons and the celebrated William Byrd. These men wrote the earliest English settings of the canticles.

*— Left —*
Henry Purcell (1659–95) gained a reputation as a composer while serving as a chorister in the Chapel Royal.

The great composers of the late 17th century were John Blow and his pupil, the young prodigy Henry Purcell. In his short life, Purcell wrote a considerable quantity of fine sacred music of a new and experimental nature.

*— Right —*
The composer Howard Goodall with Salisbury girls, who featured in his 1998 TV series *Choirworks*. Goodall is well known for his choral works as well as his TV themes, which include *Blackadder* and *The Vicar of Dibley*.

Herbert Howells (1892–1983) is commemorated in
a window of Gloucester Cathedral, for which he
wrote his magnificent setting of the canticles.

Cathedral worship was at a low ebb throughout the 18th century and little good sacred music was written. Diminished choirs depended on the vocal prowess of their individual singers, and this was reflected in the music composed at the time by Maurice Greene, William Boyce, Samuel Wesley and others, which predominantly featured solo voices. This trend continued well into the 19th century with Sir John Goss, Thomas Attwood Walmisley and Samuel Sebastian Wesley.

Around the turn of the 20th century, three fine composers emerged: Sir Hubert Parry, Sir Charles Villiers Stanford and the prolific Charles Wood. Parry's few sacred works were mostly written for special occasions and employed massive choral forces. Stanford, best known for his settings of the canticles, had a special gift for melody and harmony, and choirs today love to sing his music.

Sacred composers of the early 20th century included Edward Elgar, Alan Gray, Thomas Tertius Noble, John Ireland and, most importantly, Edward Bairstow. Later 20th-century composers included Sir William Harris, Harold Darke, Herbert Howells, Ralph Vaughan Williams, Edmund Rubbra, Kenneth Leighton and Benjamin Britten.

Cathedrals continue to commission new works by today's composers, such as Judith Weir, John Tavener, James Macmillan, Howard Goodall, Judith Bingham and Francis Grier, providing a contemporary medium for the communication of faith.

— *Above* —
Christmas is the focus for much newly composed
music. Many cathedrals' services of Nine Lessons
and Carols include a new work as well as
those that are old, familiar and loved.

— *Right* —
A roof boss at Durham
Cathedral depicts an angel
holding a shield decorated
with music.

IN THE 15TH AND 16TH CENTURIES, sacred choral music was generally presented in hand-written collections as a set of partbooks, with a separate singing part in each book. Later sets of partbooks included an organ book that gave an outline of the polyphony. The Reverend John Barnard's anthology, *Selected Church Musick*, was published in 1641, and included many of the most popular Services and anthems in use at the time.

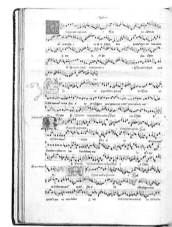

Less commonly used was the choir-book, in which the four men's parts – cantus, altus, tenor and bassus – were hand-written on two opposite pages, large enough for the whole choir to stand around and read. (Boys' voices were reserved for festal works, and were added in two parts – meanes and the higher treble.)

*— Above —*
Before the Reformation, copyists were employed by the monasteries and abbeys to write out the rich and elaborate musical settings of the sacred Latin texts.